Wit and Wisdom of
AMERICA'S FIRST LADIES

DOVER · THRIFT · EDITIONS

Wit and Wisdom of
America's First Ladies

A Book of Quotations

Edited by
JOSLYN PINE

DOVER PUBLICATIONS, INC.
Mineola, New York

DOVER THRIFT EDITIONS

GENERAL EDITOR: MARY CAROLYN WALDREP
EDITOR OF THIS VOLUME: JIM MILLER

Dedication
For Sharon, the Golden Rule personified

Bibliographical Note

Wit and Wisdom of America's First Ladies: A Book of Quotations is a new work, first published by Dover Publications, Inc. in 2014.

International Standard Book Number

ISBN-13:978-0-486-49887-4
ISBN-10:0-486-49887-5

Manufactured in the United States by Courier Corporation
49887501 2014
www.doverpublications.com

NOTE

IT MIGHT COME as a surprise to some — especially to those who associate the words "First Lady" with power, glory, and glamour — that the following excerpt from a 1901 article in *Munsey's Magazine** is nearly as true today as it was then. Entitled "Our Four Year Queens," it starts by defining the First Lady's role as "an exacting position whose duties few have fulfilled with zest and enjoyment," and continues:

> Our national boast that "any American girl may be a four years' queen" has been the source of endless day dreams under blue checked sunbonnets, and even behind dotted veils; but after a sober study of life in the White House, the glory of being First Lady in the land becomes a little dimmed. It even begins to look like very hard work; and of those who have occupied the republican throne during the past hundred and twelve years, many have approached it with reluctance and left it with relief. Some have shrunk under their own inadequacy to its duties; some have resented the sacrifice of quiet home life; many have been broken in health, too worn with a life of struggle to find pleasure in their late triumphs. A few, like Dolly [sic] Madison, have been thoroughly equal to the position, and have enjoyed its opportunities heart and soul.

Looking closely at the history of the role, a complex and often fascinating picture emerges that transcends the notion of First Lady as presidential wife — and not only in the political sense. Since several men had lost their wives before they were elected president, close female relatives or friends were often called upon to fill in as White House hostesses. For example, Thomas Jefferson had been a widower for nineteen years when he became president in 1801; and it is generally believed that his two daughters

---

* Marian West, "Our Four Year Queens," *Munsey's Magazine*, October, 1901, 907.

assumed those responsibilities for their father. However, his friend Dolley Madison is also credited with acting as Jefferson's First Lady, *before* she attained the position officially when her husband James Madison succeeded Jefferson as president.

The book at hand includes only presidential wives who served in the role, and probably more than anything attempts to present what it "feels" like to be the First Lady. And to a great extent, it inevitably reflects the role's evolution as it was changed and shaped by the times and the individuals who filled it. In the years since 1900, there were probably two factors that contributed more than any others to a transformation of the First Lady from relatively passive to very active, and even politically powerful: the explosive growth of the media; and Eleanor Roosevelt: "Greatness in a president tends to be associated with great national crises; the same is true of Eleanor Roosevelt and her ability to rise up with the American people and face the Great Depression."[†] After Mrs. Roosevelt, the job of First Lady would never be the same.

One of the greatest challenges of compiling a book of quotes is finding worthy material that can stand on its own without an immediate context. That fact, to a great extent, was a guiding principle in the selection of both the individuals and the quotations included — and excluded. So the process by necessity had to be a purely subjective one. Furthermore, as already indicated, this collection includes quotes only from First Ladies who were presidential wives.

Please note that the names of the First Ladies as they appear herein reflect the content and arrangement found on the National First Ladies' Library website (www.firstladies.org/), since there is a remarkable abundance of variations.

Because a wide variety of sources were used to assemble this compilation, spelling and punctuation have, for the most part, been modernized and standardized for the sake of clarity and consistency. And since four different references might each contain a different version of the same quote, every effort has been made to present the version closest to the spirit and substance of the original.

Joslyn Pine
May 2014

[†] John B. Roberts II, *Rating the First Ladies: The Women Who Influenced the Presidency* (New York: Citadel Press Books, 2003), xi.

CONTENTS

❧ Martha Dandridge Custis Washington ❧

Born June 2, 1731 — Died May 22, 1802
1st First Lady, 1789–1797

There were no precedents for the role Martha Washington had thrust upon her at the age of fifty-eight when her second husband became the first president of the new republic in 1789. The two were aptly considered trailblazers as together they helped define and shape what might be expected of a chief executive and his helpmate who, unlike British heads of state, had not inherited their positions by virtue of blood. Martha was known for her courage, making frequent visits to her husband's field headquarters during the Revolution, which was a means of showing her commitment to the cause as well. "Lady Washington"—as she came to be called—also distinguished herself as a superlative hostess, the first of her kind. For the sake of preserving their privacy—and at a considerable cost to posterity—Martha burned most of her correspondence with her husband before her death.

❧

I have learned from experience that the greater part of our happiness or misery depends on our dispositions and not on our circumstances. We carry the seeds of the one or the other about with us in our minds, wherever we go.

[*on being First Lady*] I live a very dull life here, and know nothing that passes in town. I never go to any public place—indeed, I am more like a state prisoner than anything else. There are certain bounds set for me which I must not depart from, and as I cannot do as I like, I am obstinate and stay home a great deal.

[*on the "ceremonies of mere etiquette" that accompanied the First Lady's role*] I sometimes think that arrangement is not quite as it ought to have been, that I, who had much rather be at home, should occupy a place with which a great many younger and gayer women would be extremely pleased. . . . I have learned too much of the vanity of human affairs to expect felicity from the scenes of public life.

1

Though I may not have a great deal of business of consequence, I have a great many avocations of one kind or another which imperceptibly consume my time.

I have been so long accustomed to conform to events which are governed by public voice that I hardly dare indulge any personal wishes which cannot yield to that.

[on Thomas Jefferson, who had been fiercely critical of her husband's policies] [He is] one of the most detestable of mankind, the greatest misfortune our country had ever experienced.

[on her husband's retirement from the presidency] The General and I feel like children just released from school or from a hard taskmaster, and we believe that nothing can tempt us to leave the sacred roof-tree again, except on business or pleasure.

I think our country affords everything that can give pleasure or satisfaction to a rational mind.

I am fond only of what comes from the heart.

✎ Abigail Smith Adams ✎
Born November 11, 1744 — Died October 28, 1818
2nd First Lady, 1797–1801

Abigail Adams is remarkable among First Ladies for being the wife of one president and the mother of another, and she was the first to live in the White House. But her formidable intellect, strong character and moral courage overshadow such facile labels. Her husband, John, considered his wife fully his equal, and as such, his key advisor on all important political issues — keeping in mind that he was on the Committee of Five who drafted the Declaration of Independence. She was fiercely opposed to slavery and voiced her objections vociferously — unafraid of exposing the hypocrisy behind the avowed principles of the American Revolution, while slavery continued to exist within the nation's borders. She was also a staunch champion of women's rights, urging her husband to include them in the governing process at a time when women didn't have the vote.

✎

These are the times in which a genius would wish to live. . . . The habits of a vigorous mind are formed in contending with difficulties. All history will convince you of this, and that wisdom and penetration are the fruits of experience, not the lessons of retirement and leisure.

[from a 1775 letter to a friend] Is it not better to die the last of British freeman than live the first of British slaves.

[from a 1777 letter to her husband] Posterity who are to reap the blessings, will scarcely be able to conceive the hardships and sufferings of their ancestors.

Merit, not title, give a man preeminence.

No man ever prospered in the world without the consent and cooperation of his wife.

[from a 1776 letter to her husband, lobbying for the protection of women when he participates in writing the laws for the young nation] In the new Code of Laws which I suppose it will be necessary for you to make, I desire you would remember the ladies, and be more generous and favorable to them than your ancestors. Do not put unlimited power into the hands of the husbands. Remember, all men would be tyrants if they could.

AND

If particular care and attention is not paid to the ladies, we are determined to foment a rebellion, and will not hold ourselves bound by any laws in which we have no voice or representation. That your sex are naturally tyrannical is a truth so thoroughly established as to admit of no dispute.

[from a 1782 letter to her husband] Patriotism in the female sex is the most disinterested of all virtues. Excluded from honors and from offices, we cannot attach ourselves to the state or government from having held a place of eminence. . . . Deprived of a voice in legislation, obliged to submit to those laws which are imposed upon us, is it not sufficient to make us indifferent to the public welfare? Yet all history and every age exhibit instances of patriotic virtue in the female sex; which considering our situation equals the most heroic of yours.

I will never consent to have our sex considered in an inferior point of light. Let each planet shine in their own orbit, God and nature designed it so. If man is Lord, woman is Lordess—that is what I contend for, and if a woman does not hold the reins of government, I see no reason for her not judging how they are conducted.

Men of sense in all ages abhor those customs which treat us only as the vassals of [their] sex.

Arbitrary power is like most other things which are very hard, very liable to be broken.

Learning is not attained by chance; it must be sought for with ardor and attended to with diligence.

I wish most sincerely there was not a slave in the province. It always appeared a most iniquitous scheme to me — fight ourselves for what we are daily robbing and plundering from those who have as good a right to freedom as we have.

I have sometimes been ready to think that the passion for liberty cannot be equally strong in the breasts of those who have been accustomed to deprive their fellow creatures of theirs. Of this I am certain: that it is not founded upon the generous and Christian principle of doing to others as we would that others should do unto us.

[answering a challenge when she enrolled one of her servants in a local school] The boy is a freeman as much as any of the young men, and merely because his face is black, is he to be denied instruction, how is he to be qualified to procure a livelihood?

Though I have been called to sacrifice to my country, I can glory in my sacrifice, and derive pleasure from my intimate connection with one who is estimated worthy of the important trust developed upon him.

[on being First Lady] I have been so used to freedom of sentiment that I know not how to place so many guards about me, as will be indispensable, to look at every word before I utter it, and to impose a silence upon myself, when I long to talk.

AND

I feel a pleasure in being able to sacrifice my selfish passions to the general good, and in imitating the example which has taught me to consider myself and family but as the small dust of the balance, when compared with the great community.

Great necessities call out great virtues. When a mind is raised, and animated by scenes that engage the heart, then those qualities which would otherwise lay dormant, wake into life, and form the character of the hero and the statesman.

If you complain of neglect of education in sons, what shall I say with regard to daughters, who every day experience the want of it?

If woman is to be council to her husband, pray train her, that he may have a learned advisor.

Every assistance and advantage which can be procured is afforded to the sons, whilst the daughters are totally neglected . . . Why should children of the same parents be thus distinguished?

[from a letter to her son, John Quincy Adams] Advising to a measure against which some objections arise, in case of failure the adviser must bear the blame.

[from a letter to her husband] You can do much service to your sons by your letters, and advice. You will not teach them what to think, but how to think, and they will then know how to act.

[remarking on English women's fashions during a trip to London] They paint here nearly as much as in France, but with more art. The head-dress disfigures them in the eye of an American. I have seen many ladies, but not one elegant one. . . . O, my country, my country! Preserve, preserve the little purity and simplicity of manners you yet possess. Believe me, they are jewels of inestimable value.

[on being presented to the Court of St. James, London] I found the Court like the rest of mankind, mere men and women and not of the most personable kind neither.

I begin to think that a calm is not desirable in any situation in life. Every object is beautiful in motion; a ship under sail, trees gently agitated with the wind, and a fine woman dancing, are three instances in point. Man was made for action and for bustle too, I believe. I am quite out of conceit with calms.

❧ Dolley Payne Todd Madison ❧
Born May 20, 1768 — Died July 12, 1849
4th First Lady, 1809–1817

The image of First Lady was enthusiastically reimagined and refined by the special endowments of Dolley Madison. She relished being treated like a celebrity and perceived new challenges to be met in the role of hostess, including redecorating the White House and dressing herself in a manner befitting a grand dame of Washington society. As the wife of Thomas Jefferson's Secretary of State, she had a head-start on her position, having assisted the third president at public functions (Jefferson was already eighteen years a widower by the time of his presidency). She was also famous for actively involving herself in charitable causes, setting a precedent for future First Ladies.

I have always been an advocate for fighting when assailed, though a Quaker.

I do not admire contention in any form, either political or civil. I would rather fight with my hands than with my tongue.

[*on refusing to flee Washington when the British invaded during the War of 1812*] I was so unfeminine as to be free from fear.

It is one of my sources of happiness never to desire a knowledge of other people's business.

What in this world can compensate for the sympathy and confidence of a mother and a sister — nothing but the tie that binds us to a good husband. Such are ours and we ought to be satisfied.

The profusion of my table so repugnant to foreign customs arises from the happy circumstance of abundance and prosperity in our country; and I shall continue to prefer Virginia liberality to European elegance.

[*on her husband, James, whom she called "The Great Little Madison"*] There was no question of his greatness, but he was also little. He was five feet, four inches tall and weighed a hundred pounds.

There is one secret, and that is the power we all have in forming our own destinies.

❧ Louisa Catherine Johnson Adams ❧
Born February 12, 1775 — Died May 15, 1852
6th First Lady, 1825–1829

Louisa Adams was notably an avid reader from her early youth, and an accomplished singer and harpist when a musical career for a woman was out of the question. She had to confront problems on many fronts when she embraced the role of First Lady. For one thing, her husband's presidency was under a cloud from allegations that his election was tainted by backroom political dealing. In addition, she suffered from a variety of ills, including severe depression, and found the White House living conditions uncongenial — cold and isolating. Further, the re-lationship between the Adamses did not flourish during the years of his presidency, exacerbated by difficulties with her rather imperious in-laws. Nonetheless, she was valiant throughout and prevailed — unsurprising for a woman who undertook a perilous six-week winter journey by carriage from St. Petersburg to Paris during Napoleon's last days, accompanied only by her seven-year-old son and two servants.

[*on her 1815 trip from Russia to France*] My journey from St. Petersburg was performed with as little uneasiness and as few misfor-tunes as could possibly be anticipated and I have really acquired the reputation of a heroine at a very cheap rate.

[*on meeting her husband's family for the first time*] Had I stepped into Noah's Ark, I do not think I could have been more utterly astonished. Do what I would there was a conviction on the part of others that I could not *suit*. . . . I was literally and without knowing it a *fine* Lady.

[*on her mother-in-law Abigail Adams*] [She was] the equal of every occasion in life.

[*from a letter to her son Charles*] When I see such women as your grandmother go through years of exertion, of suffering, and of priva-tion, with all the activity, judgment, skill and fortitude, which any man could display, I cannot believe there is any inferiority in the sexes, as far as mind and intellect are concerned, and man is aware of the fact.

[*on the White House*] That dull and stately prison in which the sounds of mirth are seldom heard.

AND

There is something in this great unsocial house which depresses my spirits beyond expression and makes it impossible for me to feel at home or to fancy that I have a home anywhere.

The more I bear, the more is expected to me, and I sink in the efforts I make to answer such expectations.

I have nothing to do with the disposal of affairs and have never but once been consulted.

[on being a woman] That sense of inferiority which by nature and by law we are compelled to feel and to which we must submit is worn by us with as much satisfaction as the badge of slavery generally, and we love to be flattered out of our sense of degradation.

✸ Sarah Whitsett Childress Polk ✸
Born September 4, 1803 — Died August 14, 1891
11th First Lady, 1845–1849

Sarah Polk was a deeply religious individual, who brought some of her beliefs with her into the White House — like abolishing dancing and not permitting business to be conducted there on Sundays. Yet despite what could have been perceived as an excessively puritanical bent, she garnered great respect among the populace as a model of propriety, and was also highly regarded by newspaper reporters of the time. She was uniquely suited to serve as her husband's personal secretary and valued political advisor, having attended in her youth the Salem Academy in North Carolina. Founded in 1772 by members of the Moravian Church, its mission was to provide a formal education to girls, when few institutions like it existed.

It is beautiful to see how women are supporting themselves, and how those who go forward independently in various callings are respected and admired for their energy and industry. . . . It is now considered proper for young ladies, when they leave school, to teach or do something else for themselves. It was not so in my young days.

[James Polk favored gold and silver over paper currency and banks, while Sarah preferred the latter] Don't you see how troublesome it is

to carry around gold and silver. This is enough to show you how useful banks are. . . . Why, if we must use gold and silver all the time, a lady can scarcely carry enough money with her.

If I should be fortunate enough to reach the White House, I expected to live on $25,000 a year, and I will neither keep house nor make butter.

When it came to actual conflict, and the lives of people with whom I always lived, and whose ways were my ways, my sympathies were with them; but my sympathies did not involve my principles. I have always belonged, and do now belong to the whole country.

The Speaker, if the proper person, and with the correct idea of his position, has even more power and influence over legislation, and directing the policy of parties than the President or any other public officer.

[on her ban of dancing in the White House] To dance in these rooms would be undignified, and it would be respectful neither to the house nor to the office. How indecorous it would seem for dancing to be going on in one apartment, while in another we were conversing with dignitaries of the republic or ministers of the gospel.

[remarking to her husband on the inherent inequality of human beings] Mr. President, the writers of the Declaration of Independence were mistaken when they affirmed that all men are created equal. . . . There are those men toiling in the heat of the sun, while you are writing, and I am sitting here, fanning myself, in this house as airy and delightful as a palace, surrounded with every comfort. Those men did not choose such a lot in life, neither did we ask for ours; we are created for these places.

❧ Mary Anne Todd Lincoln ❧
Born December 13, 1818 — Died July 16, 1882
16th First Lady, 1861–1865

Mary Todd Lincoln was another First Lady plagued by illness — including deep depression — during her tenure as presidential wife, which in her case also coincided with the Civil War. Add to it the fact that she suffered the untimely deaths of both her eleven-year-old son and her husband during those years, it is surprising to learn she was sometimes judged very harshly by members of the press of her time, and later by certain historians and biographers. Yet she possessed great personal courage, a quality that was amply tested during the war. Her accomplishments were numerous and wide-ranging, and included giving generously of her time and influence — when her intervention was vital — to ensure that wounded Union soldiers and freed slaves received the goods and services they needed. Often viewed as a tragic figure in retrospect — which in many ways she was — her legacy may be as great as her husband's in light of her own contributions and all that she did to empower him.

୭

My evil genius Procrastination has whispered me to tarry 'til a more convenient season.

Mr. Lincoln may not be a handsome figure, but people are perhaps not aware that his heart is as large as his arms are long.

[*remarking on her husband's political potential, some fifteen years before his presidency*] He is to be President of the United States some day; if I had not thought so I never would have married him, for you can see he is not pretty. But look at him! Doesn't he look as if he would make a magnificent President?

[*on her lavish spending during her husband's reelection campaign*] If he is reelected I can keep him in ignorance of my affairs; but if he is defeated, then the bills will be sent in and he will know all.

[*on the Civil War*] Clouds and darkness surround us, yet Heaven is just, and the day of triumph will surely come, when justice and truth will be vindicated. Our wrongs will be made right, and we will once more taste the blessings of freedom of which the degraded rebels would deprive us.

[*On woman's suffrage, expressing the prevailing view of her times*] As if we women in America were not in the fullest possession of every right. . . . I would recommend our strong-minded sisters to take a trip to Savoy or Saxony, where I have seen women hitched to the plough or harnessed with dogs drawing little carts through the streets.

[*responding to a charge that she was secretly aiding the Confederacy because members of her family fought for the South*] Oh, it is no use to make any defense; all such efforts would only make me a target for new attacks. I do not belong to the public; my character is wholly domestic, and the public have nothing to do with it. I know it seems hard that I should be maligned, and I used to shed many bitter tears about it, but since I have known real sorrow — since little Willie died — all these shafts have no power to wound me.

[*responding to attacks on her character following an attempt to raise funds by selling her gowns and jewelry when she was widowed*] If I had committed murder in every state in this blessed Union, I could not be more traduced. An ungrateful country, this.

[*remarks made to a close friend after the assassination*] Did ever woman have to suffer so much and experience so great a change? I had an ambition to be Mrs. President; that ambition has been gratified, and now I must step down from the pedestal. My poor husband! Had he never been President, he might be living today. Alas! all is over with me.

[*after the death of her eighteen-year-old son, Tad*] One by one I have consigned to their resting place my idolized ones, and now, in this world, there is nothing left, but the deepest anguish and desolation.

[Life teaches] by experience that power and high position do not ensure a bed of roses.

❧ Julia Boggs Dent Grant ❧
Born January 26, 1826 — Died December 14, 1902
18th First Lady, 1869–1877

Julia Grant famously enjoyed her eight years in the Executive Mansion, so much so that she wept upon leaving it. Keeping in mind that this was the post-Civil War era when Lincoln's death left her husband, Ulysses S. Grant, the nation's most visible war hero, Julia was swept along on the tide of his popularity. She spent extravagantly to make the White House the center of Washington social life, furnishing it lavishly and serving elegant dinners — featuring expensive wines and liquors — that might last up to four hours. She also made it her mission to make her family's life there as comfortable as possible, and to be a strong support to her husband.

❧

[*her stratagem to get her notably uncommunicative husband talking*] This plan I confided to several of the General's friends, who often used it with great success. I would begin to tell something with which I knew he was perfectly familiar and would purposely tell it all wrong. Then the General would say, "Julia, you are telling that all wrong," and seemed quite troubled at my incompetency. I would innocently ask, "Well, how was it then?" He would begin, tell it all so well . . .

I always knew my husband would rise in the world. I believed he would someday inhabit the highest office in the land. I felt this even when we were newly married and he was making a mere pittance in salary. My sisters used to tease me unmercifully, but you see who was correct!

I never expected to hear bad news from my General. I do not know why. I knew, I felt, he would be victorious.

The General never talked war matters with me at all. He wrote very little about the war, even after the taking of Vicksburg. I don't re- member that he wrote me any letter of exultation of joy. He was so sorry for the poor fellows who were opposed to him that he never could exult over any victory. He always felt relieved, of course, and glad that it seemed to promise to shorten the war, but he never ex- ulted over them.

I think every woman is better off at home taking care of husband and children. The battle with the world hardens a woman and makes her unwomanly.

Life at the White House was a garden spot of orchids, and I wish it might have continued forever, except that it would have deterred oth- ers from enjoying the same privilege.

❧ Lucretia Rudolph Garfield ❧
Born April 19, 1832 — Died March 14, 1918
20th First Lady, March–September, 1881
(when President Garfield was assassinated)

Lucretia Garfield's reign as First Lady was interrupted even before her husband's assassination: in May of 1881, she became deathly ill with malaria, an ordeal she fortunately survived. She was still conva- lescing at a New Jersey seaside resort when her husband was shot by a madman. Widely considered a brilliant and accomplished woman (possessed of "fine tact and faultless taste" in her husband's words), there is every indication that her legacy would have been noteworthy if her tenure had lasted more than a few months.

[on making a conscious effort to change her attitude toward baking, a task she previously disliked] It seemed like an inspiration, and the whole of my life grew brighter. The very sunshine seemed flowing down through my spirit into the white loaves, and now I believe my table is furnished with better bread than ever before; and this truth, old as creation, seems just now to have become fully mine — that I need not be the shrinking slave of toil, but its regal master, making whatever I do yield its best fruits.

The wrongly educated woman thinks her duties a disgrace, and frets under them or shirks them if she can. She sees man triumphantly pursuing his vocations, and thinks it is the kind of work he does which makes him grand and regnant; whereas it is not the kind of work at all, but the way in which and the spirit with which he does it.

It is horrible to be a man, but the grinding misery of being a woman between the upper and nether millstone of household cares and training children is almost as bad. To be half civilized with some aspirations for enlightenment, and obliged to spend the largest part of the time the victim of young barbarians, keeps one in a perpetual ferment!

Is it reasonable that the same number of stitches equally good should be worth less because taken by woman's weaker hand? Is it equitable that the woman who teaches school equally well should receive a smaller compensation than man, who is so much more able to support himself in other ways?

[on her husband's presidential inauguration] The vast concourse of people covering all the vast space in front of the Capitol was the grandest human spectacle I have ever seen.

Very many men may be loved devotedly by wives who know them to be worthless. But I think when a man has a wife who holds him in large esteem, knows that in him there is no pretense, nothing but the genuine — then he has reason to believe in his own worth.

[on the death of her husband] Oh, why am I made to suffer this cruel wrong?

We should remember greatness is not in station, but as is often said, "Act well your part, there all honor lies."

❧ Caroline Lavinia Scott Harrison ❧
Born October 1, 1832 — Died October 25, 1892
(while President Harrison was still in office)
23rd First Lady, 1889–1892

Caroline Harrison was an unusually multifaceted individual. She was a pianist and a painter who brought the art of china-painting to the White House, and designed a motif for her own set of presidential china. She supported the cause of organized labor, and was a women's rights activist who helped found the Daughters of the American Revolution (DAR) and became its president-general in 1890. In the same year, she refused to raise funds for Johns Hopkins University medical school unless it agreed to admit women. Patriotic, civic-minded and philanthropic, she was also a devoted wife and mother.

❧

[on the White House] We are here for four years . . . I am anxious to see the family of the President provided for properly, and while I am here I hope to get the present building put into good condition. . . . Very few people understand to what straits the President's family has been put at times for lack of accommodations . . . and there is no feeling of privacy.

[when her husband was accused of taking bribes] What have we ever done that we should be held up to ridicule by newspapers, and the President be so cruelly attacked, and even his little helpless grandchildren be made fun of, for the country to laugh at! If this is the penalty for being President of the United States, I hope the Good Lord will deliver my husband from any future experience.

[from her 1892 speech for the First Continental Congress of the Society of the Daughters of the American Revolution] Since this society has been organized, and so much thought and reading directed to the early struggles of this country, it has been made plain that much of its success was due to the character of the women of that era. The unselfish part they acted constantly commands itself to our admiration and example. If there is no abatement in this element of success in our

ranks, I feel sure that their daughters can perpetuate a society worthy the cause and worthy themselves.

❧ Edith Kermit Carow Roosevelt ❧

Born August 6, 1861 — Died September 30, 1948
26th First Lady, 1901–1909

Among her passions were a love of nature and good books, and she was, according to her husband, "not only cultured but scholarly." As a devoted wife and mother, Edith Roosevelt fit the template of her times, but she pushed the envelope when she became First Lady. Her famous White House renovation-redecoration project included the creation of the West Wing for the executive staff, thus freeing up the second floor as a private residence for her family of eight. She established the First Ladies Portrait Gallery and a formal display for the presidential china collection from twenty-five administrations. As a "sub rosa" diplomat, she played a significant part in the successful peace negotiations that ended the Russo-Japanese War, which earned her husband a Nobel Peace Prize.

❧

[*after McKinley's assassination, shortly after her husband succeeded him as president*] I suppose in a short time I shall adjust myself to this, but the horror of it hangs over me, and I am never without fear for Theodore.

Being the center of things is very interesting, yet the same proportions remain. When I read "The World is too much with us" or "Oh for a closer walk with God," they mean just what they did, so I don't believe I have been forced into the "first lady of the land" model of my predecessors.

[*on her husband, post-presidency*] I want him to be the simplest American alive after he leaves the White House; and the funniest thing to me is that he wants to be also and says he is going to be, but the trouble is he has really forgotten how to be.

[*on FDR, a fifth cousin of Teddy Roosevelt*] We expected Franklin Roosevelt to take us out of the mud when he went into office, but he has led us into the mire.

A lady's name should appear in print only three times: at her birth, marriage, and death.

One hates to feel that all one's life is public property.

❧ Helen Louise "Nellie" Herron Taft ❧
Born June 2, 1861 — Died May 22, 1943
27th First Lady, 1909–1913

Helen Taft was an unusually ambitious woman of many talents who found a worthy outlet in the job of First Lady. She fearlessly ignored many of the barriers imposed by the social codes that had formerly prevailed at the White House, so that a far greater diversity of individuals (in terms of race and rank, especially) would have access there. It was "Nellie" who facilitated the change in presidential transportation from horse-drawn vehicle to automobile, and she defiantly served alcohol at the White House despite fierce outcries from prohibitionists. One of her most notable accomplishments was West Potomac Park, a public park she wanted everyone to enjoy, which was planted with thousands of cherry trees — including a sizeable donation from the City of Tokyo — that remain to this day. She was morally and politically a progressive who used her considerable influence to champion underdogs of all stripes, focusing her attention most particularly on factory workers' rights and women's suffrage.

❧

[*on Inauguration Day*] I stood for a moment over the great brass seal, bearing the national coat of arms, which is sunk in the floor in the middle of the entrance hall. "The Seal of the President of the United States," I read around the border, and now — that means my husband!

[*on being First Lady*] I had always had the satisfaction of knowing almost as much as he about the politics and intricacies of any situation. I think any woman can discuss with her husband topics of national interest. I became familiar with more than politics. It involved real statesmanship.

I believe in the best and most thorough education for everyone, men and women . . . My idea about higher culture for women is that it makes them great in intellect and soul, develops the lofty conception of womanhood; not that it makes them a poor imitation of a man. . . .

No fundamental superiority or inferiority between the two appears plain to me. The only superiority lies in the way in which the responsibilities of life are discharged.

Why is it so very rare in a man and woman to be simply intimate friends. Such a friendship is infinitely higher than what is usually called love, for in it there is a realization of each other's defects, and a proper realization of their good points without that fatal idealization which is so blind and, to me, so contemptible. . . . From my point of view a love which is worthy of the name should always have a beginning in the other.

✎ Ellen Louise Axson Wilson ✎

Born May 15, 1860 — Died August 6, 1914
(while President Wilson was still in office)
28th First Lady, 1913 — August 6, 1914

Before gaining fame as a First Lady, Ellen Wilson was already an accomplished artist in the American Impressionist style. Many of her paintings won awards and were featured in gallery exhibitions. But she is equally notable for being a reformer who brought her political influence to bear on opposing child labor and helping the mentally ill. She also sought to improve housing in the largely black-populated slums of the nation's capital, taking congressmen on tours so they could witness first-hand the deplorable living conditions. Eventually her efforts led to the so-called "alley clearance bill," which forms an enduring part of her legacy of reform. As for her value to her husband, President Wilson wrote of her: "No president but myself ever had exactly the right sort of wife!"

[on being First Lady] A person would be a fool who lets his head be turned by externals; they simply go with the position.

AND

Nobody who has not tried can have the least idea of the exactions of life here and of the constant nervous strain of it all.

I am naturally the most unambitious of women and life in the White House has no attractions for me.

I wonder how anyone who reaches middle age can bear it if she cannot feel on looking back that, whatever mistakes she may have made, she has on the whole lived for others and not for herself.

[from a letter to her husband] I love you more, a thousand times more than life. There is no standard great enough to measure my love.

❧ Edith Bolling Galt Wilson ❧
Born October 15, 1872 — Died December 28, 1961
28th First Lady, 1915–1921

As President Wilson's second First Lady, Edith Wilson proved a controversial figure both then and now, involving herself in affairs of state far more than her predecessor, leaving her little time for the pursuit of special causes. But this was largely not a matter of choice as the special circumstances of her husband's presidency conspired to make her America's first woman president — as she is sometimes referred to, often as a reproach. From October 1919 to March 1921, after Wilson suffered a massive stroke and his true condition was kept secret, she became a powerful behind-the-scenes political figure whose avowed goal was to protect her husband and his position. Considering that until the passage of the twenty-fifth amendment to the Constitution in 1967, there was no plan in place in the event of a president's sudden disability in office, her behavior may be viewed more judiciously in that context.

❧

[on being the President's confidante] From the first he knew he could rely on my prudence, and what he said went no further.

[speaking of the time in 1919 when her husband was incapacitated by a stroke impelling her to act on his behalf "sub rosa"] I studied every paper, sent from the different secretaries or senators, and tried to digest and present in tabloid form the things that, despite my vigilance, had to go to the President. I myself never made a single decision regarding the disposition of public affairs. The only decision that was mine was what was important and what was not, and the *very* important decision of when to present matters to my husband.

AND

I am not thinking of the country now, I am thinking of my husband.

✽ Florence Mabel Kling DeWolfe Harding ✽
Born August 15, 1860 — Died November 21, 1924
29th First Lady, 1921–1923

Florence Harding had three favorite causes she championed during her tenure as First Lady. One was a passionate commitment to women's rights and equality with a view to empowering them as independent individuals not bound by the conventions of their sex. In light of her feminist advocacy, it is fitting that she was the first president's wife to vote for her husband for president — his 1920 election having followed the passage of the nineteenth amendment to the Constitution in 1919. Florence was also a staunch activist on behalf of disabled veterans of World War I, and lobbied tirelessly for their welfare. Finally, she was outspoken on the subject of the humane treatment of animals and lent her considerable influence to the cause. It is sad to note that her legacy has been dimmed by the Teapot Dome scandal that tainted the Harding administration.

✽

I'd rather go hungry than broil a steak or boil potatoes. I love business.

[*on her success as a businesswoman in her hometown of Marion, Ohio*] I was allowed to progress in the business world as fast and as far as I could. And remember, we were small-town folks, and small towns' conventions are more hidebound.

The time has passed for discussion about the desirability of having the women actively participate in politics. They are in politics, and it is their duty to make their participation effective.

[*on the occasion of Madame Marie Curie's visit to the White House*] She has been the associate and partner of her husband in their great work of scientific research, and it seemed to me that their relationship was peculiarly ideal and of the sort that must point the way for all of us to the ideal family relationship of the future.

[*on women and physical fitness*] The part that women play in the world has been greatly changed even in my own generation. It has broadened and enlarged, and we will be wise if we recognize that a larger consideration for the health and physical advancement of girls will better fit them for the role they must assume.

Cruelty begets cruelty, hardness towards animals is certain to breed hardness towards our fellow man. Of this, I am very sure from both observation and analogy, the converse is just as true. That is why I am always willing to give every encouragement to humane causes.

Men and women assumed a great responsibility when they made the animals their servants or their friends; they assume the responsibilities for the comfort and happiness of the dumb creatures that have given up so much of their capacity for happiness through a natural life, in order to serve their masters. So I always think of our duty to the animals.

I have only one real hobby — my husband.

[My husband] has a winning way about him that has always disarmed enmity. He can differ sharply with a man — but always without offending him.

I know what's best for the President. I put him in the White House. He does well when he listens to me and poorly when he does not.

I am content to bask in my husband's limelight, but I cannot see why anyone should want to be President in the next four years. I can see but one word written over the head of my husband if he is elected and that word is Tragedy. [*Warren Harding died while still in office, albeit of natural causes.*]

❧ Grace Anna Goodhue Coolidge ❧
Born January 3, 1879 — Died July 8, 1957
30th First Lady, 1923–1929

Grace Coolidge was far and away one of the most popular First Ladies, considered warm, charming and accessible, particularly in comparison with her stern and taciturn husband. Her status as such is even more remarkable in light of the fact that her husband limited her activities — especially anything even remotely political. Despite these restraints, Grace publicly enjoyed walking and hiking, and was an avid baseball fan — dubbed the "First Lady of Baseball" by a Boston Red Sox official. She loved animals and frequently appeared in public with one of her numerous four-legged companions, including her pet raccoon, Rebecca. Her involvement in the White House encompassed both the domestic and the ceremonial realms; and she sought to preserve its historical legacy by bringing back items that had previously been removed — like Abraham Lincoln's bed. Prior to her marriage, she had taught at the Clarke School for the Deaf in Massachusetts, and as First Lady, pursued her commitment to the education and needs of the disabled.

[on being First Lady] If I had manifested any particular interest in a political matter, I feel sure I should have been properly put in my place.

AND

There was a sense of detachment. This was I, and yet not I. This was the wife of the President of the United States and she took precedence over me. My personal likes and dislikes must be subordinated to the consideration of those things which were required of her. In like manner, this man at whose side I walked was the President of our great country; his first duty was to its people.

AND

Daily I am impressed anew with the responsibility and opportunity which has been given me. In no sense does it overwhelm me, rather does it inspire me and increase my energy and I am so filled with the desire to measure up.

To me, the House of the Presidents is sacred ground, hallowed by the memories of those great men whom our country has chosen for the high office. To live in it is to live in a shrine.

I was more proficient in setting up and operating miniature tracks and trains on the dining room floor, than in receiving and entertaining guests in the drawing room . . . we New England women cling to the old way and being the President's wife isn't going to make me think less about the domestic things I've always loved.

Although my husband has moved up, it makes no difference in our mode of living. Why should it? We are happy, well, content. We keep our bills paid and live like everyone else.

[remark made to a prominent society woman excited about being seated next to Coolidge — nicknamed "Silent Cal" — at a dinner] I'm sorry for you. You'll have to do all the talking yourself.

I have such faith in Mr. Coolidge's judgment that if he told me I would die tomorrow morning at ten o'clock, I would believe him.

Marriage is the most intricate institution set up by the human race. . . . The woman is by nature the more adaptable of the two and she should rejoice in this and realize that in the exercise of this ability she will obtain not only a spiritual blessing but her own family will rise up and call her blessed.

Many a time, when I have needed to hold myself firmly, I have taken up my needle. It might be a sewing needle, knitting needles, or a crochet hook—whatever its form or purpose, it often proved to be as the needle of the compass, keeping me to the course.

There is a song from one of our not new musical comedies about girls, which says something about "the short, the fat, the lean, the tall; I don't give a rap, I love them all." This is the way I feel about people, and I have been fortunate in being placed where I had an opportunity to gratify my taste by meeting great numbers of them.

[from a letter to a friend, on leaving the White House] Please treat me rough when I get home, and kick me about a bit so I'll realize I'm human.

[on her husband's plans for retirement] I haven't any idea what he has in mind. I always did like the unexpected and am waiting with intense interest the next jump.

I was born with peace of mind. It is a matter of inheritance, training, and experience.

Surely sixty should be the "Age of Wisdom," but I often think that the older I grow the less wise I am.

[on widowhood] I am just a lost soul. Nobody is going to believe how much I miss being told what to do.

❧ Lou Henry Hoover ❧
Born March 29, 1874—Died January 7, 1944
31st First Lady, 1929–1933

Lou Hoover was a First Lady notable for more than one "first." She was a geologist by profession and one of the first women to earn a degree

*in the field. She was the first to catalog the White House collection
of historical items, which would prove an invaluable resource for the
restoration projects of future administrations. A passionate outdoors-
woman, she conceived of the idea of a presidential retreat in the form
of Camp Rapidan, the antecedent to Camp David, in the Blue Ridge
Mountains, and supervised its construction down to the most minute
detail. Despite all her accomplishments, the fallout from the Great
Depression cast a shadow on this energetic First Lady, who continued
to serve lavish White House dinners while so many in the nation were
starving.*

॰

I enjoy campaigning because my husband makes the speeches and I
receive the roses.

I majored in geology at college, but I have majored in Herbert Hoover
ever since.

I believe that even after marriage it is possible for a woman to have
a career. . . . The modern home is so small there is little work to do.
The baby? It isn't a baby for long. There is no reason why a girl should
get rusty in her profession during the five or six years she is caring for
a small child.

I have done nothing extraordinary, nor anything more than a woman
should do for the man she loves. I have been deeply interested in Mr.
Hoover's work and have tried to be of whatever assistance I could. My
chief hobbies are my husband and our sons.

Only with the help of a perfectly trained and good-natured staff, was
it possible to make the domestic wheels of the White House move
smoothly and silently.

The independent girl is a person before whose wrath only the most
rash dare stand, and, they, it must be confessed, with much fear and
trembling.

Bad men are elected by good women who stay away from the polls on
election day.

Women should get into politics. They should take a more active part
in civic affairs, give up some of their time devoted to pleasure for
their duty as citizens. Whether we are wanted in politics or not, we are

here to stay and the only force that can put us out is that which gave us the vote. The vote itself is not a perfect utility. It is perfected in the way it is used.

[from a 1931 radio broadcast, during the Great Depression] My plea is that our most important duty is to find when, how, and where people need help. The winter is upon us. We cannot be warm, in the house or out, we cannot sit down to a table sufficiently supplied with food, if we do not know that it is possible for every child, woman, and man in the United States also to be sufficiently warmed and fed.

❧ Anna Eleanor Roosevelt Roosevelt ❧
Born October 11, 1884 — Died November 7, 1962
32nd First Lady, 1933–1945

Regarding Anna Eleanor Roosevelt Roosevelt: genealogically speaking, as the daughter of Elliott Roosevelt, younger brother of Theodore, she was the latter's niece; she was related to her husband Franklin as a fifth cousin, once removed — meaning a difference of one generation. She was reform-minded from a very young age, to some extent consciously emulating her Uncle Teddy. She always lived her activist principles, as was amply demonstrated in a myriad of ways: during World War I, by her activities on behalf of the American Red Cross and her volunteer work at Navy hospitals; championing the needs and rights of the disadvantaged — women, children, minorities, the poor; publicly and privately abhorring racial discrimination; and the list of her humanitarian achievements goes on and on. She was also a trusted political adviser and steadfast wife to her husband throughout the twelve years of her tenure as First Lady, when her special gifts were applied to great effect through two national crises: the Great Depression and World War II.

❧

Campaign behavior for wives: Always be on time. Do as little talking as humanly possible. Lean back in the campaign car so everybody can see the President.

[on being First Lady] It was hard for me to remember that I was not just "Eleanor Roosevelt," but the "wife of the President."

AND

There isn't going to be any "First Lady of the land." There is just going to be plain, ordinary Mrs. Roosevelt. . . . I never wanted to be the President's wife, and I don't want it now. You don't quite believe me, do you? Very likely no one would — except possibly some woman who had had the job.

People can be brought to understand that an individual, even if she is a President's wife, may have independent views . . . but actual participation in the work of government we are not yet able to accept.

I have the memory of an elephant. I can forgive, but I cannot forget.

It is better to light a candle than curse the darkness.

It is often the people who refuse to assume any responsibility who are apt to be the sharpest critics of those who do.

Ambition is pitiless. Any merit that it cannot use it finds despicable.

A little simplification would be the first step toward rational living.

The giving of love is an education in itself.

One of the great secrets for making the most of one's time and energy is to put yourself completely into what you are doing at the moment. Live in the present, not in what is yet to come.

Looks alone do not make one attractive. If you cultivate your mind and your spirit, you can have charm, which is far more important than looks.

The basic thing which contributes to charm is the ability to forget oneself and be engrossed in other people.

A woman is like a tea bag; you never know how strong it is until it's in hot water.

Self-pity and withdrawal from the battle are the beginning of misery.

Work is always an antidote to depression.

I think women are often superior to men in their intuition about people, in their executive ability when they are handling detailed work, and in their ability to subordinate themselves to a cause or to another individual if they think that is the way to serve a cause.

Women have one advantage over men. Throughout history they have been forced to make adjustments. The result is that, in most cases, it is less difficult for a woman to adapt to new situations than it is for a man.

The happy home will be the one in which the woman is not considering that her husband's success is measured by his salary.

It is hard for a man to side against his mother even if he feels his wife is right.

I think if psychiatric care were available to all at small cost a great many people might obtain help when they found themselves faced with difficulties in their daily lives which now result in broken homes.

Teachers are more important than anything except parents in the lives of children.

Children, rich and poor, are the wealth of a nation. Their hands and their heads, as they grow to maturity, are going to determine what happens in every country in the world.

I believe very strongly that it is better to allow children too much freedom than too little.

We do not have the old-fashioned idea of making a child do a thing simply because he is told to do it. From his earliest days we teach him the reason back of what is asked of him.

For a child there is no wound deeper than that made by belittling laughter, and no wall more impenetrable than that built by habitual ridicule.

I would bend every effort if I were bringing up children today to teach them moderation in all things.

I don't think children owe their parents any gratitude. It is love, not obligation, which brings about warm and happy relations within families.

The child who is aware that his parents do not tell him the truth will assume that the practical method is to lie. The child who sees his parents sacrifice everything for material possessions will not believe that spiritual values are important.

I think, at a child's birth, if a mother could ask a fairy godmother to endow it with the most useful gift, that gift should be curiosity.

I wish I were young so that I did not have to consider so many sides of every subject. It is so much easier to be enthusiastic than to reason.

Too many of us stay walled up because we are afraid of being hurt. We are afraid to care too much, for fear that the other person does not care at all.

You must do the things you think you cannot do.

It isn't enough to talk about peace. One must believe in it. And it isn't enough to believe in it. One must work at it.

I think the art of relaxing comes with self-discipline. You learn to assume a relaxed position, you learn to control your mind and stop it going around in circles.

The purpose of life, after all, is to live it, to taste experience to the utmost, to reach out eagerly and without fear for newer and richer experience.

Only those who love really live, in spite of the pain loving so often brings.

I would not judge a man's character by his belief or unbelief. I would judge his character by his deeds; and no matter what he said about his beliefs, his behavior would soon show whether he was a man of good character or bad.

Do what you feel in your heart to be right — for you'll be criticized anyway. You'll be damned if you do, and damned if you don't.

Unless we make of ourselves persons whom we like, with whom when occasion demands, we can live pleasantly in solitude, we are poorly equipped for social life in any community.

It is not fair to ask of others what you are not willing to do yourself.

No one loves two people in exactly the same way, but one may love two people equally and yet differently. And if you love one person very much you will love another person perhaps even more because you have learned how to love and what love can mean.

Great minds discuss ideas; average minds discuss events; small minds discuss people.

Death is unnatural when it comes to the young, but with age it is normal and inevitable and, like everything else that has been inevitable in life, becomes easier to accept.

The most unhappy people in the world are those who face the days without knowing what to do with their time.

Happiness is not a goal; it is a by-product.

It is not more vacation we need — it is more vocation.

Nothing alive can stand still. Life is interesting only as long as it is a process of growth; or, to put it another way, we can grow only as long as we are interested.

I have only two remedies for weariness: one is change and the other is relaxation.

It takes as much energy to wish as it does to plan.

It is a pity that we cannot have the experience that comes with age in our younger days, when we really need it.

Unless time is good for something, it is good for nothing.

No one can make you feel inferior without your consent.

Without self-respect, few people are able to feel genuine respect for others.

If you will forget about yourself, whether or not you are making a good impression on people, what they think of you, and you will think about them instead, you won't be shy.

The only things one can admire at length are those one admires without knowing why.

[an observation made at age fourteen] No matter how plain a woman may be, if truth and loyalty are stamped upon her face all will be attracted to her.

The only advantage of not being too good a housekeeper is that your guests are so pleased to feel how very much better they are.

One of the secrets of using your time well is to gain a certain ability to maintain peace within yourself so that much can go on around you and you can stay calm inside.

When life is too easy for us, we must beware or we may not be ready to meet the blows which sooner or later come to everyone, rich or poor.

If life were predictable it would cease to be life, and be without flavor.

Old age has deformities enough of its own. It should never add to them the deformity of vice.

Never allow a person to tell you no who doesn't have the power to say yes.

Too little attention is paid to the passive sins, such as apathy and laziness, which in the long run can have a more devastating and destructive effect upon society than the others.

Because it is easier to say "I can't" than "I can," many people go through life unaware of untapped strength, even untapped ability.

It always seemed to me that there must be some kind of immortality, because it would be such a wasteful performance otherwise.

When will our consciences grow so tender that we will act to prevent human misery rather than avenge it?

The future belongs to those who believe in the beauty of their dreams.

✌ Elizabeth Virginia "Bess" Truman ✌
Born February 13, 1885–Died October 18, 1982
33rd First Lady, 1945–1953

Bess Truman may be fairly described as a very reluctant First Lady. She preferred to be out of the public eye and avoided contact with the press whenever possible. She embraced her role as primarily a social one and busied herself with the activities of hostess. Members of the White House staff spoke highly of her as a warm and witty individual. She involved herself in the more traditional social endeavors of her predecessors like the Red Cross and the Girl Scouts. First and foremost, she presented herself as a wife and mother, and was said to have been a valued advisor to her husband—behind the scenes. Each summer she fled the White House for Missouri, and she was unabashedly delighted when her husband announced his retirement from politics.

A woman's place in public is to sit beside her husband, be silent, and be sure that her hat is on straight.

[*on being First Lady*] We are not any one of us happy to be where we are, but there's nothing to be done about it except to do our best — and forget about the sacrifices and many unpleasant things that bob up.

Harry and I have been sweethearts and married more than forty years — and no matter where I was, when I put out my hand, Harry's was there to grasp it.

I'm no different from anyone else. If I don't have a [library] card, I can't take out these books.

I've liked lots of people 'til I went on a picnic jaunt with them.

❧ Mamie Geneva Doud Eisenhower ❧
Born November 14, 1896 — Died November 1, 1979
34th First Lady, 1953–1961

Mamie Eisenhower was one of the most admired women of her era and one of the most popular First Ladies of the twentieth century, despite being relatively low key and traditional in her approach to the role. It was a sensitive time for the nation, still recovering from World War II and having newly emerged as a world power because of it. The picture of normalcy and serene domesticity that the president and his family projected was largely a result of Mamie's persona — a middle-class woman with middle-class values as embodied in everything from her wardrobe choices to her taste in TV shows like I Love Lucy. *But she also brought a world of valuable experience with her from having been a military wife that greatly enhanced her abilities and achievements as presidential wife.*

[*on being an Army wife*] I've lived in everything from shacks with cracks to palaces.

[*as a new occupant of the White House*] I've just had the first good night's sleep I've had since we've been in the White House. Our new bed finally got here, and now I can reach over and pat Ike on his old bald head any time I want to.

[*on being First Lady*] Of course, being mistress of the White House is a terrific responsibility, and I am truly grateful for my Army wife training.

[*on the importance of women's involvement in Civil Defense*] Any housewife may be tomorrow's heroine. . . . It is difficult in the midst of our present day lives, filled with so many home and community activities, to believe that an atomic attack could happen here. It can happen. We must be prepared.

Ike runs the country, and I turn the lamb chops.

As an American woman I have always valued my right to pretty clothes.

❧ Jacqueline Lee Bouvier Kennedy Onassis ❧
Born July 28, 1929 — Died May 19, 1994
35th First Lady, 1961–November 22, 1963
(when President Kennedy was assassinated)

In the history of First Ladies, Jacqueline Kennedy occupies a unique place as a national icon, an American version of royalty. The timing of her tenure was fortuitous since it coincided with a media on the rise as a force in society, and she was a perfect subject for its focus, what with her youth and beauty, her fashion sense, her aristocratic pedigree, and her personal agenda — using the power of politics to benefit art. In 1962, her most notable TV appearance, A Tour of the White House with Mrs. John F. Kennedy, was enormously popular and she was soon seen on the covers of numerous magazines. In the course of her famous restoration of the presidential mansion, the position of White House Curator and the White House Historical Association were created to maintain it as a living museum ad infinitum. Finally, her courage, grace, and dignity helped console and sustain a grief-stricken nation when her husband was assassinated.

❧

[*on life lived in the public eye*] I feel as though I have just become a piece of public property. It's really frightening to lose your anonymity at thirty-one.

The one thing I do not want to be called is First Lady. It sounds like a saddle horse.

It's such an adjustment to go from private life to constant surveillance.

I think the best thing I can do is to be a distraction. A politician lives and breathes politics all day long. If he comes home to more table-thumping, how can the poor man ever relax?

[on being a wife to JFK] I brought a certain amount of order to his life. We had good food in our house — not merely the bare staples that he used to have. He no longer went out in the morning with one brown shoe and one black shoe on.

If you bungle raising your children, I don't think whatever else you do well matters very much.

Children have imagination, a quality that seems to flicker out in so many adults. That is why it is such a joy to be with children.

People have too many theories about rearing children. I believe simply in love, security, and discipline.

Once you have a child, you don't think of yourself so much but of the generation ahead. Any sacrifice is made with joy.

One could raise a child with one's left hand but why let it be such a casual operation when the responsibility in bringing more to the child's world is the greatest joy for the parent. There are so many little ways to enlarge this world. Love of books is the best of all.

It never hurts a child to read something that may be above his head. Books written down for children often do not awaken a dormant curiosity.

What is sad for women of my generation is that they weren't supposed to work if they had families. What were they to do when the children were grown, watch the raindrops coming down the windowpane?

[on her brother-in-law, Bobby] People of a private nature are often misunderstood because they are too shy and too proud to explain themselves.

[on her courtship by JFK] I'm the luckiest girl in the world. Mummy is terrified of Jack because she can't push him around at all.

You have to have been a Republican to know how good it is to be a Democrat.

All the talk over what I wear and how I fix my hair has amused and puzzled me. What does my hairdo have to do with my husband's ability to be President?

Being a fashion leader is at the very bottom of the list of things I desire.

I don't think there are any men that are faithful to their wives.

[in response to her husband's complaint about one of the many problems that besieged him, in this case, "What in the hell am I ever going to do about air pollution?"] It's very simple, my dear. Get the Air Force to spray our industrial centers with Chanel No. 5.

The most important thing for a successful marriage is for a husband to do what he likes best and does well. The wife's satisfaction will follow.

There are two kinds of women: those who want power in the world, and those who want power in bed.

One day in a campaign can age a person thirty years.

[on being a public figure] When you get written about a lot, you just think of it as a little cartoon that runs along at the bottom of your life — but one that doesn't have much to do with your life.

[on the charge of extravagance from her husband] I have to dress well, Jack, so I won't embarrass you. As a public figure you'd be humiliated if I were photographed in some saggy old housedress. Everyone would say your wife is a slob and refuse to vote for you.

Politics is in my blood. I know that even if Jack changed professions, I would miss politics. It's the most exciting life imaginable. . . . You get used to the pressure that never lets up, and you learn to live with it as a fish lives in water.

If Jack didn't run for President, he'd be like a tiger in a cage.

[her reaction when she first toured the White House] Oh, God. It's the worst place in the world. So cold and dreary. A dungeon like the Lubyanka [a Soviet prison]. It looks like it's been furnished by discount stores. I've never seen anything like it. I can't bear the thought of moving in. I hate it, hate it, hate it.

When I first moved into the White House, I thought, I wish I could be married to Thomas Jefferson, because he would know best what should be done to it. But then I thought, no, Presidents' wives have an obligation to contribute something, so this will be the thing I will work hardest at myself.

Everything in the White House must have a reason for being there. It would be a sacrilege merely to "redecorate" it—a word I hate. It must be *restored*—and that has nothing to do with decoration. That is a question of scholarship.

The White House is an eighteenth- and nineteenth-century house and should be kept as a period house. Whatever one does, one does gradually, to make a house a more lived-in house with beautiful things of its period. I would write fifty letters to fifty museum curators if I could bring Andrew Jackson's inkwell home.

I don't understand it. Jack will spend any amount of money to buy votes, but he balks at investing a thousand dollars in a beautiful painting.

It takes an awful lot of effort to make everything look effortless.

Happiness is not where you think you find it. I'm determined not to worry. So many people poison every day worrying about the next.

There will never be Camelot again.

❧ Lady Bird [Claudia Alta] Taylor Johnson ❧
Born December 22, 1912 — Died July 11, 2007
36th First Lady, 1963–1969

Lady Bird Johnson had already taken a special interest in the lives of the First Ladies before she unexpectedly became one herself. Her study of the subject helped her infuse the role with a new level of professionalism, as was amply demonstrated by her advocacy of Beautification, a nationwide program that equated environmentalism with humanism, and led to a dizzying array of stellar and enduring achievements. A staunch feminist who had herself earned a degree in the arts and later another in journalism, she was also vocal in her support of higher education for women. She fully embraced LBJ's War on Poverty and played a vital role as the honorary chair of the original Project Head Start for disadvantaged preschool children.

The First Lady is an unpaid public servant elected by one person — her husband.

[*on the White House*] History thunders down the hall.

In the war on poverty, as we have raised the curtain on some of our most blighted conditions, we have come to know how essential beauty is to the human spirit. You can find the human craving for it in small things and large.

[*on Project Head Start*] [This is] the big breakthrough we have been seeking in education . . . a lifeline to families lost in a sea of too little of everything — jobs, education, and most of all perhaps — hope.

Children are apt to live up to what you believe of them.

I have always been a natural tourist. Lyndon used to say I kept "one foot in the middle of the big road." Wherever I go in America, I like it when the land speaks its own language in its own regional accent.

Our challenge is to seize the burdens of our generation and make them lighter for those who follow us.

Woman can no longer afford to concern herself only with the hearth — any more than man can afford to concern himself only with his job.

The confusion of roles for women today is still very real. The strains are real. But many women have been able to master the confusion.

I would like to see young women from the outset consider their lives in the longer perspective — looking to the time after your children are grown when you will still have time for an ongoing part in the human drama.

I've really tried to learn the art of clothes, because you don't sell for what you're worth unless you look well.

[*on becoming First Lady*] If I had known that this was going to happen to me, I would have changed my nose and my nickname.

I had the idea that people were supposed to love me because I had an interesting mind, a kind heart, and a warm smile. I thought that Lyndon's emphasis on clothes and appearance was the wrong system of values. He used to say that a lot of the people that I met would only see me once, and that the opinion they would form would persist. He wanted them to have a good opinion of me. By the world's rules, he was right. I was wrong.

Every politician should have been born an orphan and remain a bachelor.

I've had a long love affair with the environment. It is my sustenance, my pleasure, my joy. Flowers in a city are like lipstick on a woman, it just makes you look better to have a little color.

Though the word beautification makes the concept sound merely cosmetic, it involves much more: clean water, clean air, clean road-sides, safe waste disposal and preservation of valued old landmarks as well as great parks and wilderness areas. To me . . . beautification means our total concern for the physical and human quality we pass on to our children and the future.

I believe that one of the great problems for us as individuals is the depression and the tension resulting from existence in a world which is increasingly less pleasing to the eye. Our peace of mind, our emotions, our spirit — even our souls — are conditioned by what our eyes see. Ugliness is bitterness.

I know that the nature we are concerned with ultimately is human nature. That is the point of the beautification movement, and that finally is the point of architecture. Winston Churchill said, "First we shape our buildings, and then they shape us." The same is true of our highways, our parks, our public buildings, the environment we create. They shape us.

Once a woodland glade bows to the bulldozer, it is lost forever. An aroused citizenry is the greatest safeguard.

The environment is where we all meet; where all have a mutual interest; it is the one thing all of us share. It is not only a mirror of ourselves, but a focusing lens on what we can become.

Some may wonder why I chose wildflowers when there are hunger and unemployment and the big bomb in the world. Well, I, for one, think we will survive, and I hope that along the way we can keep alive our experience with the flowering earth. For the bounty of nature is also one of the deep needs of man.

Every man has a thirst to leave his footprints on untrammeled sand. I hope it will always be so and that we will always provide it. It has been said that wilderness is the miracle that man can tear apart but cannot reassemble. . . . At every beach, there are new shells to find, new dunes to paint.

There is much the government can do and should do to improve the environment. But even more important is the individual who plants a tree or cleans a corner of neglect. For it is the individual who himself benefits, and also protects a heritage of beauty for his children and future generations.

Where flowers bloom so does hope.

[An] understanding of nature should be a part of every child's education, for if our young people grow up with an awareness of the beauty around them, they are much more likely to protect it.

The modern world with all its turbulence and problems has taught us many things, but none more clearly than this: Education is the engine of progress.

Education is a loan to be repaid with the gift of self.

The well-written word is man's most useful instrument — the way the superior mind catches human experience and reshapes the insignificant particulars into a pattern that has meaning for us all.

Any committee is only as good as the most knowledgeable, determined and vigorous person on it. There must be somebody who provides the flame.

It is through sharing the benefits of our way of life that our way of life will survive.

Everything we do begins at home. Each of us is action-sprung from what nurtures us.

[on the enormity and weight of her husband's responsibilities] It is odd that you can get so anesthetized by your own pain or your own problem that you don't quite fully share the hell of someone close to you.

We want a world at peace, a security based on mutual trust. We want our children to live in a country — in a community — which bases its actions among its citizens on fair play, fair play for all, not because it is political or expedient, but because it is morally right.

I think discipline is something children want. They feel cherished because of it and would feel lonely and abandoned if they were not disciplined.

One of the profound challenges of our civilization is to preserve the oldest and most cherished of our values in the midst of the newest achievements of our genius and growth. It is to ensure that the spiritual needs of the people are not lost and submerged by abundance and progress.

The sound of laughter marks the soaring spirit.

The enlightened woman of today bears love not only for her one man, but for mankind, not only for her children, but for all children.

Children are likely to live up to what you believe of them.

History will judge [America] not by our abundance or by our mighty arms or our vast influence — but by our people: their values, their wisdom, their skill, and their happiness.

Science and time and necessity have propelled us, the United States, to be the general store for the world, dealers in everything. Most of all, merchants for a better way of life.

Success has many faces; it need not be circumscribed by a title, a job, a cause. Success is not always "getting." It is more often "giving." It does not consist of what we do, but rather in what we are. Success is not always an accomplishment. It can be a state of mind.

I feel sometimes Lyndon thinks I am more capable than I am — which in a way makes me grow to be a little more capable.

Perhaps no place in any community is so totally democratic as the town library. The only entrance requirement is interest.

Art is the window to a man's soul. Without it, he would never be able to see beyond his immediate world; nor could the world see the man within.

While Washington can rally together the leaders and experts, it is — after all — back in our hometowns where inspiration becomes action and results take shape.

Sometimes silence is the greatest sin.

It is far easier to cut down a tree than to grow one. It is far easier to pollute a river than to restore it. It is far easier to devastate a flowering countryside than to make it bloom again.

Your land of promise is in your own backyard.

Keep America beautiful. Plant a tree, a shrub, or a bush.

I'll know I am growing old when I no longer thrill to the first snow of the season.

ᴥ Elizabeth Ann "Betty" Bloomer Warren Ford ᴥ
Born April 8, 1918 — Died July 8, 2011
38th First Lady, 1974–1977

Betty Ford was another unexpected First Lady — when Nixon resigned from the presidency post-Watergate — who made her brief tenure count. Breaking with the traditional reticence of the role, she was fearlessly honest and outspoken on many of the most inflammatory issues of the day, including abortion (pro-choice), women's rights, and divorce (she was herself a divorcée); and openly discussed the breast cancer that necessitated her mastectomy in 1974, shortly after her husband took office. It is likely that her very public airing of the subject saved countless lives as many women sought mammograms or treatment when they probably wouldn't have otherwise. After leaving public office, she again made headlines when she admitted to her dependence on alcohol and prescription drugs, focusing attention on another life-threatening disease, which ultimately led to the creation of the Betty Ford Center for the treatment of addiction.

Don't compromise yourself. You are all you've got.

Being ladylike doesn't require silence.

[on being First Lady] [It's] much more of a twenty-four-hour job than anyone would guess. . . . Now that I realize what they've had

to put up with, I have new respect and admiration for every one of them.

I do not believe that being First Lady should prevent me from expressing my ideas.

I don't feel that because I'm First Lady, I'm very different from what I was before. It can happen to anyone. After all, it has happened to anyone.

[on promoting the Equal Rights Amendment to her husband] If he doesn't get it in the office in the day, he gets it in the ribs at night.

[from her speech on the occasion of President Ford's designation of 1975 as International Women's Year] We have come a long way, but we have a long way to go — part of that distance is within our own mind. . . . Let us work to end the laws and remove the labels that limit the imagination and the options of men and women alike. Success will open hearts and minds to new possibilities for all people.

Any woman who feels confident in herself and happy in what she is doing is a liberated woman.

When I say I've had an ideal marriage, I'm not just talking about physical attraction, which I can imagine can wear pretty thin if it's all a couple has built on. We've had that and a whole lot more.

It's always been my feeling that God lends you your children until they're about eighteen years old. If you haven't made your points with them by then, it's too late.

When someone asks you how you stand on an issue, you're very foolish if you try to beat around the bush — you just meet yourself going around the bush the other way.

[on coming to terms with her drinking problem] My makeup wasn't smeared, I wasn't disheveled, I behaved politely, and I never finished off a bottle, so how could I be alcoholic?

At one time during my husband's administration I made the smart-aleck remark that a First Lady ought to be paid, she had a full-time job, and I'm not sure I wasn't right.

❧ Eleanor Rosalynn Smith Carter ❧
Born August 18, 1927
39th First Lady, 1977–1981

Rosalynn Carter was an energetic and productive presidential wife who genuinely enjoyed being First Lady and gave her all to the job. A full political partner with her husband, she was actively involved with a wide range of domestic and foreign issues including, first and foremost, a sweeping reform of the mental health system, women's rights, programs for the elderly, the Camp David Accords between Egypt and Israel, aid for Cambodian refugees—and the list goes on. While she wasn't highly rated by the public during her tenure, this "steel magnolia," as she was called by one reporter, ranked third—behind Eleanor Roosevelt and Lady Bird Johnson—on an historians' list of the ten most effective First Ladies.

I don't think that there is any doubt that the First Ladies have some influence on their husbands, because they are close to them, they talk with them all the time, they have the presidents' ear.

[*when her husband admitted in a* Playboy *interview that he'd "looked on a lot of women with lust"*] Jimmy talks too much but at least people know he's honest.

Choose how you will spend your time, select a few key projects, stand by your convictions, and ignore the criticisms.

If we have not achieved our early dreams, we must either find new ones or see what we can salvage from the old.

❧ Anne Frances "Nancy" Robbins Davis Reagan ❧
Born July 6, 1921
40th First Lady, 1981–1989

Nancy Reagan abandoned her acting career—appearing in eleven films from 1949 to 1956—for marriage, and never looked back. Theirs was a true romance, and as First Lady, she took it upon herself to see her primary role as protector, especially after the assassination attempt on her husband's life in 1981. There were also two social causes espe-

cially close to her heart: the war on drugs, especially among the young, and the Foster Grandparent program that encouraged older Americans to become involved in the lives of disadvantaged children.

[her advice to future First Ladies] Once you're in the White House, don't think it's going to be a glamorous, fairy-tale life. It's very hard work with high highs and low lows. Since you're under a microscope, everything is magnified, so just keep your perspective and your patience.

[on her movie career] Most of [my films] are best forgotten.

I must say acting was good training for the political life which lay ahead for us.

[on her Just Say No to Drugs campaign] Drugs take away the dream from every child's heart and replace it with a nightmare, and it's time we in America stand up and replace those dreams.

[on her Foster Grandparents program] It benefits both sides: children, who need love, and grandparents, elderly people, who need to feel wanted.

[recalling the assassination attempt on her husband's life] Everyone remembered the funny things Ronnie said after he was hit. No one seemed to want to remember how close he came to dying.

I think it's an important, legitimate role for a First Lady to look after a President's health and well-being. And if that interferes with other plans, so be it. No First Lady needs to make apologies for looking out for her husband's personal welfare . . . The First Lady is, first of all, a wife.

For eight years, I was sleeping with the President, and if that doesn't give you special access, I don't know what does.

Did I ever give Ronnie advice? You bet I did . . . I was the only person in the White House who had no agenda of her own except helping him.

[on her husband's thoughtfulness] What can you say about a man who on Mother's Day sends flowers to his mother-in-law, with a note thanking her for making him the happiest man on Earth?

❧ Barbara Pierce Bush ❧
Born June 8, 1925
41st First Lady, 1989–1993

Barbara Bush was a very popular and widely admired First Lady who possessed a warm maternal persona and a forthright manner spiced with wit that automatically put people at ease. During her tenure, she promoted volunteerism by living it, and brought national attention not only to the problem of illiteracy in America, which led to the launching of the Barbara Bush Foundation for Family Literacy, but also to the special needs of indigent and homeless families and people with AIDS.

[on becoming First Lady] My mail tells me that a lot of fat, white-haired, wrinkled ladies are tickled pink.

The First Lady is going to be criticized no matter what she does. If she does too little. If she does too much. And I think you just have to be yourself and do the best you can.

Some people give time, some money, some their skills and connections, some literally give their life's blood. But everyone has something to give.

I think togetherness is a very important ingredient to family life. It's a cliché and we use it too much, but I think for a husband and wife, the way to stay close is to do things together and to share.

I married the first man I ever kissed. When I tell this to my children, they just about throw up.

[from a 1990 Wellesley College commencement address] Who knows? Somewhere out in this audience may even be someone who will one day follow in my footsteps, and preside over the White House as the President's spouse. . . . I wish him well!

The American Dream is about equal opportunity for everyone who works hard. If we don't give everyone the ability to simply read and write, then we aren't giving everyone an equal chance to succeed.

At the end of your life, you will never regret not having passed one more test, not winning one more verdict or not closing one more deal. You will regret time not spent with a husband, a friend, a child or a parent.

❧ Hillary Diane Rodham Clinton ❧
Born October 26, 1947
42nd First Lady, 1993–2001

Hillary Clinton is another First Lady who followed her own agenda and demonstrated boundless energy when it came to fulfilling her role. In her first week in office, she became the head of the President's Task Force on Health Care Reform, an effort that eventually had to be abandoned, largely due to adverse political pressures. Still, she brought public awareness to the problem of those without health care, and pressed on nonetheless to successfully spearhead other legislation that benefitted disadvantaged children and families especially. She was a New York State senator from 2001 to 2009, and pursued a run for the 2008 presidency, until Barack Obama bested her in the primary race. In 2009 she became the sixty-seventh secretary of state, visiting more countries than any of her predecessors.

❧

Every moment wasted looking back, keeps us from moving forward.

Every child needs a champion.

[*on heading up the President's Task Force on Health Care Reform*]
Every President who has touched [health care] has got burned in one way or the other because the interests involved are so powerful.

AND

Until we have everybody in the system, we will not be able to control health care costs.

Fear is always with us, but we just don't have time for it.

It is a tribute to American women that, coming from different social and economic backgrounds, from many different geographical regions, and with diverse educational preparation, each First Lady served our country so well. Each left her own mark, and each teaches us something special about our history.

The challenge is to practice politics as the art of making what appears to be impossible, possible.

I have read enough history to know that no matter what I do, I will be fair game.

Take criticism seriously, but not personally. If there is truth or merit in the criticism, try to learn from it. Otherwise, let it roll right off you.

I believe that a worthwhile life is defined by a kind of spiritual journey and a sense of obligation.

[Eleanor Roosevelt] was one of those rare people who strike that elusive balance between "me" and "we." Between our rights and expectations as individuals and our obligations to the larger community.

We are determined to channel the currents of change toward a world free of violent extremism, nuclear weapons, global warming, poverty, and abuses of human rights, and above all, a world in which more people in more places can live up to their God-given potential.

I think women's role in politics will continue to grow. I don't hold with the idea that women are better than men in public life, but most women bring different experiences into the public arena. I hope in the years to come not only will more women participate, but women will try to change the content of politics so we will be more focused on what we can do for children, for instance, and win more support for families.

It is no longer acceptable to discuss women's rights as separate from human rights. . . . Women's rights are human rights once and for all.

The difference between a politician and a statesman is that a politician thinks about the next election while the statesman thinks about the next generation.

✎ Laura Lane Welch Bush ✎
Born November 4, 1946
43rd First Lady, 2001–2009

Among the wide range of her achievements as First Lady, first and foremost was her advocacy on behalf of education and libraries. Her love of education started with a love of reading, and so the two pursuits became inextricably bound in her own agenda for social progress. She initiated a National Book Festival in Washington, D.C., promoted No Child Left Behind, and instituted several programs designed to draw new candidates into the teaching profession — including Troops to Teachers, to help members of the military embark on a new and meaningful career. Formal tributes to her efforts include UNESCO's honorary Ambassadorship for its Decade of Literacy and the federally funded Laura Bush 21ˢᵗ Century Librarian Program, which is part of the Institute of Museum and Library Services.

Politics is a people business. I like people.

The role of the First Lady is whatever the First Lady wants it to be.

I have a lifelong passion for introducing children to the magic of words. I was a public school teacher and I know what a difficult and rewarding job teaching is.

I think a great teacher is priceless. I think teachers have a more profound impact on our society and culture than any other profession.

Education can help children see beyond a world of hate and hopelessness.

The power of a book lies in its power to turn a solitary act into a shared vision. . . . As long as we have books, we are not alone.

∽ Michelle LaVaughn Robinson Obama ∽
Born January 17, 1964
44th First Lady, 2009–incumbent

Early on as First Lady, Michelle Obama — the mother of two young daughters — dubbed herself Mom-in-Chief, thus drawing criticism from those who seemed to interpret the concept as antifeminist. But it was indeed a misinterpretation since she has implicitly made the moniker part and parcel of her favorite cause as embodied in "Let's Move!" — which is to protect all children from the specter of childhood obesity and foster healthy nutrition. She also helps support service members and their families with opportunities and resources through "Joining Forces," an organization she formed with Dr. Jill Biden.

❧

At the end of the day, my most important title is still "Mom-in-Chief." My daughters are still the heart of my heart and the center of my world.

For the first time in my adult life, I am proud of my country because it feels like hope is finally making a comeback.

[on Obama's presidential win in 2008] This time, we listened to our hopes, instead of our fears. . . . this time, we decided to stop doubting and to start dreaming. . . . this time, in this great country . . . we committed ourselves to building the world as it should be.

The truth is, in order to get things like universal health care and a revamped education system . . . someone is going to have to give up a piece of their pie so that someone else can have more.

Finding balance has been the struggle of my life and my marriage, in being a woman, being a professional, being a mother. . . . What women have the power to do, through our own experiences, is to push that balance out into the culture. If people are happier, and they're more engaged, and they have jobs they can value that allow them to respect and value their homes, that makes the home life stronger.

[Barack and I] want our children — and all children in this nation — to know that the only limit to the height of your achievements is the reach of your dreams and your willingness to work for them.

[on "Let's Move," her initiative to tackle the problems of childhood obesity and poor nutrition] This is one of those issues that has no party. It has no race. It has no socioeconomic boundaries. This is about our kids.

I want to leave something behind so that we can say, "Because of this time that this person spent here, this thing has changed." And my hope is that that's going to be in the area of childhood obesity.

We can make a commitment to promote vegetables and fruits and whole grains on every part of every menu. We can make portion sizes smaller and emphasize quality over quantity. And we can help create a culture — imagine this — where our kids ask for healthy options instead of resisting them.

It's not enough just to limit ads for foods that aren't healthy. It's also going to be critical to increase marketing for foods that are healthy.

[Barack's] always asking: "Is that new? I haven't seen that before." It's like, why don't you mind your own business? Solve world hunger. Get out of my closet.

Women in particular need to keep an eye on their physical and mental health, because if we're scurrying to and from appointments and errands, we don't have a lot of time to take care of ourselves. We need to do a better job of putting ourselves higher on our own "to do" list.

Women are definitely under a lot of pressure, but I think it's important to remember that to look good, you have to feel good. I look at my mom at seventy-four and see how beautiful she looks and how wonderful she is with our daughters and with me and my husband — and I want that for myself when I'm her age.

We should always have three friends in our lives — one who walks ahead, who we look up to and we follow; one who walks behind us, who is with us every step of our journey; and then, one who we reach back for and bring along after we've cleared the way.

One of the lessons I grew up with was to always stay true to yourself and never let what somebody else says distract you from your goals. And so when I hear about negative and false attacks, I really don't invest any energy in them, because I know who I am.

[on the rationale for her White House mentoring program for girls] You don't always see was what it took for many of us to get to where we are today. You don't always see the thousands of hours that were spent studying or practicing or rehearsing, the years spent working for that promotion, the hammers used to break glass ceilings. All of them — every last one of them — had someone in their lives who took the time to encourage them and to inspire them. None of us are here on our own.

Do not bring people in your life who weigh you down. And trust your instincts . . . good relationships feel good. They feel right. They don't hurt. They're not painful. That's not just with somebody you want to marry, but it's with the friends you choose. It's with the people you surround yourselves with.

You may not always have a comfortable life and you will not always be able to solve all of the world's problems at once, but don't ever underestimate the importance you can have because history has shown us that courage can be contagious and hope can take on a life of its own.

Barack and I were raised with so many of the same values: that you work hard for what you want in life; that your word is your bond and you do what you say you're going to do; that you treat people with dignity and respect, even if you don't know them, and even if you don't agree with them.

The arts are not just a nice thing to have or to do if there is free time or if one can afford it. Rather, paintings and poetry, music and fashion, design and dialogue, they all define who we are as a people and provide an account of our history for the next generation.

Policies that support families aren't political issues. They're personal. They're the causes I carry with me every single day.

The truth is that Brown vs. Board of Education isn't just about our history, it's about our future. . . . There's no court case against believing in stereotypes or thinking that certain kinds of hateful jokes or comments are funny. So the answers to many of our challenges today can't necessarily be found in our laws — these changes also need to take place in our hearts and in our minds.

All of us driven by a simple belief that the world as it is just won't do . . . have an obligation to fight for the world as it should be.

INDEX